old shul

poems

pinny bulman

Ben Yehuda Press
Teaneck, New Jersey

Published by Ben Yehuda Press
122 Ayers Court #1B
Teaneck, NJ 07666

http://www.BenYehudaPress.com

To subscribe to our monthly book club and support independent Jewish publishing, visit https://www.patreon.com/BenYehudaPress

Jewish Poetry Project #35   **http://jpoetry.us**

Ben Yehuda Press books may be purchased at a discount by synagogues, book clubs, and other institutions buying in bulk. For information, please email markets@BenYehudaPress.com

ISBN13 978-1-953829-55-9

23 24 25 / 10 9 8 7 6 5 4 3 2 1   20231006

For Melissa, my soulmate,
and for Ariella & Avishai,
our nachas

In memory of
all the old shuls of Washington Heights
now shuttered

L'iluy nishmas
my dad, Aaron Bulman, z'l,
forever my favorite poet

old shul

beyond the shul

1: old shul

hanging on

light coming reluctantly through
the taped up colored windows in
their rusting metal cages
obscuring the scratched empty benches
the undercarpet places where the floor
breaks like tired voices
reciting worn prayers
later thrown over streetlamps
like old sneakers
fraying   holed
maybe a little dangerous
but hanging on.

shadows

as the evening prayers cast
shadows on stained plastic windows
we godspoke to the rhythm
of backfiring buses
and the strains of merengue
from the neighboring building
to which half the empty room
was subconsciously swaying

on leaving we
steadied ourselves
by the side fence
voices mute with exile
as the rats found shelter
stuffing themselves into cracks
like prayer notes

and a little girl
hoisted herself
up onto the fence bars
pointing to
the color topped needles
scattered like toys
suddenly left.

impr0v1sati0n

we kept updating the street-side announcement board
long after the sermons lost
their titles
when the few of us left
already knew the prayer times
and any other jews who chanced upon it
too busy figuring out where they took a wrong turn
to care about the timing of afternoon services on a tuesday

it became its own ritual
fumbling with the rusty lock
half-frozen fingers seeking a winter's grip
to slide out the thick plastic cover
long detached from the metal frame
the awkward trot with the
heavy board down the block and
into the shul where generations of
letters and numbers in various stages of yellowing
disintegration jumbled together in
a primordial language of babel

as more letters broke
became extinct altogether
we had to improvise
an upside down backwards 7 standing in for L
1 and 3 touching to make a B
until the entire board became an improvisation
replacing something broken
that needed to be announced

even if mostly obscured
behind the growing number of scratchitti tags
on the plastic cover
that told the passersby everything
they really needed to know.

old shul

minyan

our hope became habit
waiting for the tenth
like a tired love   fading slow

our lives less certain
with each prayer
whispered like a secret
no one wants to hear anymore.

pinny bulman

sign

shaky lettering on
cardboard
hung on the bent gate
by the side entrance:

please do not go
to the bathroom here.

snow

no chimney
the shul shivers
looks wistfully at a
building in the
distance idly taking
an early morning smoke

the naked wrinkled roof
gives a weary shrug
as the dirt white blanket
hides its mismatched patches
settles on its castle-like parapets
leaning as though to
huddle for warmth
once defenses against
something that overpowered
long ago.

pinny bulman

trees

most blocks had two
maybe three
leaning awkwardly toward the buildings
like estranged relatives posing
for a forced photo

but this block was
passed over
as with so much else,
perhaps too much blood
on the doorpost

and when the wind blew
the only rustle
came from the tired steel bridge
swaying slowly
as though rocking the traffic
to sleep.

leaking

water leaking
from
a roof
onto siddurim with mold-softened edges
their prayers for rain
misunderstood

aluminum pan bailing buckets
placed over spreading carpet stains
become mini-mikvahs
for small pieces of ceiling plaster
the occasional dead roach
our tashlich sins

as the upper waters
return to the lower
in a sort of de-creation
no one here is saved

this water does not split
or spring fresh from parched desert rock

but as the sharp
ratatattat
of water slapping aluminum
becomes the soft sound
of rain to puddle
there is no need for prayer

only to listen.

pinny bulman

god once

there
in the torah ark
amidst the tarnished silver
the scrolls yellowing like nicotine-stained fingers
long since unable to
steady as a
drawstring is groaningly pulled and
the drunken matted curtain jerks
open with fits and
starts

no mountain carved fire tablets
spirit creator gathering thunder

just there
one time
unnoticed by the
bored voices uninterested
in melody, the worn
words themselves idly
focused on a dirty jagged
fingernail scratching the side of
a scarred nose

and i too
there
with nothing to say
no new psalms of awe
prayer poems of desire
kinos of anger
despairing loneliness
regret

sometimes it's enough
just to stand in a moment of mute belief
the tent's threshold
until a pulley moves in reverse
and the length of drawstring that settles back into view
measures a newly frayed
absence.

pinny bulman

havdalah

whoever donated the
silver modernist spice holder
could not have imagined
the way my dad
could make it look
like a hungry space alien
opening and
closing its clove-filled mouth
with a ridiculous
whispered growl daring me
to keep a straight face in
front of the congregants as
i sang the start to
each week with
choked back
laughter.

squish

shabbos hung summer limp
could not be wrung out until
the sighting of three medium-sized
waterbugs in the downstairs social hall
moving across the buckled rug
like inverse shooting stars
in a tattered grease-stained sky

as a kid i would usually
hang back in fearful disgust
watch as others strode
like big-footed gods
across that crumb-strewn universe
extinguishing those frantic brown suns

and in these moments
i'd try to reflect on transition
and death
the way they so often mingled but
it was hard to be existential when
there was a contest to see
who could make the
loudest squish.

pinny bulman

facing west

we prayed facing west,
at our backs
a crowded history
occasionally coughing apologetically
asking for the page number

and in front
high above the ark
a series of twelve
stained glass square panels
neither tribes nor prophets

an exile's vision
of promised land as
otherworldly landscape
curving shapes
in shades of crimson violet
a messianic dream of quiet abstraction
several panels hinting
at an ancient city
distant enough to render
questions of habitation
nationality   religion
irrelevant

but when shabbos exhaled
sun setting behind the neighboring apartment building
the darkness that fell across the twelve panels
was a hebrew darkness
moving from right to
left in a language of gentle erasure
until the moment when
nothing left to see
we turned east
and exited the shul
into night.

blessing the moon

they sent me out
after saturday night services
to check for a sliver
of new moon to
bless,
somewhere above the tall
cans of el presidente sweating in
low beach chair cup holders,
overlooking the group of kids
hiding the fire hydrant spray with
a bucket, strategically removed
when a car passed with
carelessly rolled down window,
the gleeful kids excitedly scattering
as the soaked driver stepped out
waving a metal bat,
his threatening curses drowned out
by the slap of dominos to wood and
the loud booms of M80s
thrown off rooftops,
adding percussion
to the cranked up car speaker merengue
shaking the hips of the stoopgirls
in tight shorts who
scared me and sometimes
showed up in my dreams

i slunk to the curbside edges
worried that some of the night laughter
was directed at the jewish kid in
wrinkled old man suit
looking up for a glimpse of
moon i may as well have been from
a skinny curve of white

boy searching for something to bless,
and more,
praying for someone streetside
to look up and
bless me.

shofar

her building had no need for an entrance buzzer
let alone a doorman
the front door easily forced open,
last year's only greeting a confused glance
from a man with urine-soaked pants
slumped against a wall
whispering secrets to the broken floor tiles

but this visit was different
an office desk incongruously planted in the graffitied lobby
where the confused glance now came from
a professional looking woman in uniform

the moment of mutual gawking ended
with the flashing of a federal badge
as she began writing in her notepad
three white males, jewish
one middle-aged, beard, glasses (father)
two teens, look younger than stated age (sons)
dark wrinkled suits, scuffed dress shoes
quarter-sized soup stain on adult's red tie
no IDs
refused to sign entry log (religious reasons)
carrying small bag, inside: one ram's horn(!)
requesting to visit elderly woman, apt. 4J

the agent whispered into a walkie talkie
and waved us on
her gaze following us up the narrow staircase where
i distracted myself counting
the burn marks on the sections of
banister still attached

pinny bulman

we found her apartment quickly
its entrance distinguished
by the lack of police tape
and a small mezuzah camouflaged on the doorframe
by a coat of paint
indiscriminately applied years ago

it troubles me that i can no longer picture her
as she lay mute
in that frail, bedbound, final new year
but i can remember her face softening
when my dad spoke to her
in his broken yiddish

and when he lifted
the shofar to his lips
its ancient sound echoed through the dirty hallways
back to a time when human sacrifice
could still be averted
by a voice from above
calling a name.

old shul

tashlich

we threw our sins
our hidden shames
off the neighboring bridge,
watching as they momentarily settled on the water's surface
before submerging in the erratic
currents pulling them out toward the harbor

they say the river's not as polluted anymore
but i know better
i know what's been thrown
sometimes most of me
decomposing among the bodies of those who forgot to let go
who lost their ability to shed
like cats out of season
but without the nine lives

at night when
the bridge lights trembled in the sky like floating lanterns
shivering with the autumn wind in a season of fallings
that's when i took her hand
held her close
as we sang each other through the long walk back to
solid ground.

pinny bulman

ledge

between steps and wall
a thin
strip
of floor
that forgot to end,
just continued on
oblivious to everything else
dropping away

on a dare i would inch across,
white bits of wall plaster
and my dark dress pants
clinging to each other
with held breath

and memories of a crowd
myself among them
looking up at a building ledge across the street
the mood turning ugly
some placing bets
shouting for blood,
each of us studying the physics
measuring our distances

but when it's me on the ledge
with so much and so
little at stake
i freeze

everything else dropping away
except a choice.

smelling salts

yom kippur turned sour early afternoon
the sweat-stained air grimacing
at the perfunctory efforts of
the AC compressor fan whose on/
offs marked a slow unending
passage of pages,
an ironic comment on life's
brevity

the old men would look around for victims
pull out their small
glass bottles of smelling salts and
in the absence of fainters
wave us kids over unsuspecting
cackling with glee at our
muffled shrieks
quickly averted noses
unaware that their dentured fasting breath
had a pungency the
salts could only dream of

until evening when the wind would shift
rustling the old men
now shuffling up
to open the torah ark in
their sneakered feet,
ready to run

and the stink of our final desperate prayers
rose straight up to the sky
like an ancient sacrificial offering
to a noseless god.

pinny bulman

sukkah

the size of the stone
to be thrown
from a building roof
onto the alleyway sukkah
below
should be no less than
the size of an olive
these are the words of beis hillel

beis shammai say
no less than
the size of an egg
lest those below think
it was an accident
perhaps a passing wind

upon leaving the sukkah
rabbi yehuda would say
may our children be blessed
in the coming year
to dwell in a rooftop shul sukkah
somewhere beyond the mishnaic exile
a parent's oversized sweater wrapped tight
against the evening chill off the river

lulled to sleep, head on forearm
by the ebb and flow
of adult laughter
mixing with the bridge traffic tides,
dreams restless
with the sounds of mournful truck horns
calling to something ancient
in the waters below.

genizah

there were dark places in shul
behind a heavy half-stuck metal door
that screamed when opened
cutting through the prayers like a rusty sacrificial knife

the door was labeled emergency exit
beyond it broken bookcases
falling slowly down a windowless corridor
toward the steep set of uneven stairs with partially
detached handrail

i once avoided these places
their floors littered with torn
phrases from crumbling prayer books,
forgotten piyyutim liturgizing our nightmares

but now i go back
candle and feather in hand
searching for my history's fragments
so many lost

i hold them tenderly
before burying them inside myself,
deep beneath words
and the silences that follow.

pinny bulman

startle

the hurried silence
of early morning smokers
disturbs the distances
of dirtied prayers
perched like pigeons on crowded rooftop-edges
daring G-d to startle
movement to ash-filled sky
rasping psalms
in a blackened language
while contemplating a fall
into the fingernail dug crevices
of tongueless ovens
expelling early morning smoke
into a hurried silence.

picky

i was picky
could afford to be in those days when
the bodega bins overflowed with cheap exuberance
like penny slots
and the sidewalks were littered
with half-smoked loosies
at all the bus stops

the shul was upset
by my skinny refusals,
the way my nose twitched
at its whisky sardine breath
its herring juice fingers
wagging disapproval

and i didn't understand until
i learned that its closest relative
had been in europe during the war,
last seen alive in dachau
its once grand architecture
shrunk to shtiebel size
splintered beams visible
behind frail walls
rooting in the frozen
mud for a fallen
crumb.

pinny bulman

swastika

as graffiti it wasn't
much to look at
a few crude lines in marker
down a flight of side stairs
on the door of the shul's emergency exit
almost hidden amidst the other usual tags

nothing like the nearby mural
a half-block explosion of swirling colorful pain
depicting presidential patriarchs found on paper money
exploring their role as slave owners
perpetuating the country's economy of racism,
all this on the side of a bank

but it was the small anonymous nazi pinwheel
that pushed me to action
to go out that night armed
with a black sharpie,
squeeze through the bent bars
of the locked side gate to
blot out the swastika
mark up the area with jewish stars
my own ancient tag

soon after,
the shul door was repainted
the mural wall whitewashed

in fact it's been years since that bank
was torn down
the shul soon to follow,
and when i die
the only thing standing between
that swastika and complete oblivion
will be this poem

but i am of a people who understand
the importance of tagging history,
keeping a memory of all that needs
to be erased.

pinny bulman

rock

no one was hurt
and the graffiti-covered window
anyway needed replacing
and it was, at least,
only one rock
and it could have been
a random act
and yet

i no longer remember
the size of the rock
or the pattern of glass shards on prayer books,
the colors they reflected in the suddenly
uncensored early evening light
of the fading shabbos

it's the nervous excitement that stayed with me
of a personal kristallnacht
a connection to lives of tattooed numbers
fragile as windows
of a history i can point to
and say
mine.

after the rock

the windows were barred
caged
as though guilty
for all that was shattered,
their jailors in uneasy truce
with the tired window frames
rattling warnings to the oblivious traffic

my mind would follow the metal-dappled light
back to the ceiling of my childhood bedroom
the diamond patterned streetlight shadow
of a security gate
keeping the fire escape
at bay

lock and hinges rusted
as an added precaution
denying the possibility that
danger could ever
come from
within.

pinny bulman

fall

when a fall isn't chosen
but treads with desperate softness
through an unlocked shul door
like a late season
that sneaks up from behind
and pushes hard

the latest in a series of falls
most visible from the vantage point of
bruised wrinkled cheek
pressed to cold cracked wood floor
rifling through memories, vulnerabilities
like an early morning junkie through pockets

two dimes
a penny
an old receipt
and pieces of a diabetic cookie
broken against the hard muttered curses
jarring the few arthritic hebrew murmurers
out of their usual achy stupor
and then gone,
along with the loose change
and solid ground

the rabbis say when a torah scroll falls
one must fast 40 days,
but if an old man
is pushed to the ground
in an old shul

no one talks about this.

breaking shabbos to call the cops

it wasn't when
the guys from the block gathered
to give some purse-snatching outsider
a beatdown

no, that line was
crossed when J announced
he was going back to get his
nail-studded bat.

pinny bulman

shots fired

for years we heard
but they were just out of
sight around a
corner in the
background like the rhythmless bang
of the radiator unnoticed until
that sleepless night it's suddenly
all you can hear

probably just a car backfiring
our parents would pretend
but we knew that even the newer models
couldn't sneak onto rooftops
down fire escapes
couldn't shout demands
trigger finger trembling
in the building lobby

we tiptoed past the kids
playing jump rope with police tape
and tried not to stare
at the jagged holes left
in family albums,
the ones almost left
in ours

and so my walk to shul became
    a zig
zag
    with unsuspecting
pedestrians
        garbage piles
lampposts
       my cover

and in years since
i've relearned to walk a straight line but
haven't yet shaken
the target on my back.

shabbos money

pocket change
a postwar survivor's minhag
minimum of three coins
jingled loudly in shul
each sound of forbidden metal
removing the wings of an angel

the dollar bills came later
when the killing was random
silent as the one angel in which we all still believed,
the one that didn't know your name
to call it from above
but when it came demanding sacrifice
you'd better have something
to give.

no parking

don't know why the city bothered
to occasionally plant a no parking sign
in front of the shul,
almost immediately plucked
as though a rare wildflower
perhaps presented to some puzzled lover
oh honey, you shouldn't have

anyway there was no
need for a sign,
everyone who lived in the area
knew not to park there

the cars on the bridge side
of the shul got off easy
just roughed up
maybe punched in the eye,
we crunched our way down that block
the little bits of glass
like sparkly gravel

but the spot in front
of the shul was reserved
for the cars with license plates already removed,
we blushed to see them stripped naked
tried to look
away as they were
decomposed to skeleton

those rusty bones haunted us
their restless apparitions reflected
in my parents' eyes
when their college friends started making suburban excuses
stopped driving in to visit

and i became secretly glad we never
owned a car because life was
simpler with nothing
to lose.

dogs

i loved t.v. dogs
the frisky ones that caught frisbees
sometimes dragged you out of a burning building
but the neighborhood turned them mean
taught them to snarl and snap

we learned to stay away from the pitbulls
using the playground swings as chewtoys
crossed the street when they fought on our block
spectators cheering from their seats
on the church side stoop

it was harder to avoid their droppings
left everywhere from sidewalks to building lobbies
as though traditional ways of marking territory
were no longer good enough

the sidewalk next to the shul was especially bad
seemingly zoned for use as canine dumping ground
and i always seemed to take a wrong step

i used to tiptoe through
pretending that block was a minefield
until a school assembly
where we were asked to collect charity for
jewish families in iran
back then at war with iraq

we were told of jewish children our age
sent to the front
made to walk in front of the soldiers
through fields with actual mines buried
as though traditional ways of marking territory
were no longer good enough

pinny bulman

and so i guiltily stopped pretending
tried not to daydream so much
taught myself to step carefully through life
with deliberate stealthy caution
like a cat.

karate

local ethnic turf wars were long since
lost by attrition, old stories of
a time when we were still
a threat, not yet
demoted to
curiosity

some still fought
carried knives, learned martial arts
i took one free intro karate class in the shul basement
and promptly became a tactical pacifist
grandmaster of quiet
avoidance, a silent witness stalking
the streets with pent up words just waiting to
explode.

sentries

at the corner payphone up our block the old disheveled
stooped man, large shopping bag filled with yellowed papers,
shouted in a wild gesticulating german into the dial tone
occasionally pausing to spit at passersby
who quickened their pace down the hill
their relief at escaping tempered by the sight of
the tall silent one at the other corner
standing by the church with a blank
menacing stare, hands clasped behind his back
except when greeting jews with a
heil hitler salute as we passed
until tired of ignoring, excusing
arik laid him out on the sidewalk
and a sad-eyed woman walked up to the payphone
to whisper soothingly in the old man's ear
take him gently by the arm
and slowly lead him home.

bikes

the streets were all downhill
back when a subway elevator could lift us
from the lowest to
highest point in our universe

some rode in packs
reckless sidewalk
             racing
weaving
                          pedestrian
wild
        slalom

i rode alone
suffered my wipeouts quietly
victimless
until an elderly man taught us
we could kill

sometimes at the top of a steep hill
i still picture a stained borcelino hat continuing on its way
down to shul unaware of
the grounded head suddenly bare

but some skills can't be forgotten
and all i can do
is brush myself off
remount
and hold on tight as i pick up speed.

rats

it was always my job to go first
being the oldest and marginally less afraid
my brother waiting at the top of the block
i pounding the sidewalk with my shoes
to keep them at bay
until reaching the side entrance
i held open
to spare my brother
the extra half-second

meir was no athlete but
he could be surprisingly quick and
i've never seen him move quite as fast as
he did during those sprints down 179th street
on those rat-infested early shul mornings

only one time did i
pretend to hold the door closed

for a moment
until his face taught me
there are some fears you don't play with
even if it is your
kid brother.

first love

that she was
double my 13 years
not yet converted to judaism
living with her fiancé
only deepened my shabbos crush
made it safely impossible

the shul brushed itself off in those days
shaved its stubble
the old fluorescent bulbs buzzing
winking me encouragement as i pursued her
amidst the stale crackers and herring
of the post-prayer kiddush

until the sunday
my mom sent me with a package to
her apartment

she was barefoot
wearing tight blue jeans
and invited me in
offered me a glass of water
amidst the modernist furnishings
the collection of jazz albums

my words blushed st
umbled ov
er each
other as
i fled

paced the neighborhood
ending up at the shul
brickface crumbling

front gate sagging
revealing too much
like an unintentionally lewd old man
who forgot to put on his suspenders

that's when i realized
i was on my
own.

reach

back then
growing up meant
being able to
jump high enough to reach the low ceiling
under the women's balcony

the older kids would
sneak up on each other
and brush the area over
someone's head
to watch the white ceiling particles
settle on hair
clothing
carpet
like an extreme case of dandruff

and the annoyed exclamations
of the elderly men
meant as little to us
as the word asbestos
or the prayers we replaced with daydreams
that years later
we can no longer reach.

pinny bulman

recycling

those empty glass bottles weren't
much to look at
slipping through fingers
to lay askew on
the sidewalk next to
bodies slumped against
the sides of apartment buildings
like fallen gargoyles
stonestill
even when a young foot
sent one skittering
to feel the guilty thrill
of shatter

we laughed when
the shul super started collecting empties
planted dozens facedown in the strip
of dirt along the building edge
as though hoping for liquor trees
to spring up where little else would
until we realized
he was plugging up the rat holes

and when we exited the shul
after evening services in winter
the streetlights would twinkle across
the frozen glass bottoms
like all the stars
we couldn't see.

liquor tree

i heard it first
a soft ethereal chiming
drifting lonely and lost down audubon
in a season when
everything the other trees had
to offer had fallen
months before

it must have taken
hours to string each
of those bottles from
the bare branches,
curved glass shapes swaying
slowly in the cold breeze
spilling a riot of shadow and color
onto the broken sidewalk
with each passing headlight

the mood shifting
when the wind picked up
and chime turned to clank
the disoriented bottles stumbling
awkwardly against each other
like drunken ornaments
as i hurried away reminded
that all things of beauty
must shatter.

　　　　　pinny bulman

pacing

i moved through prayer
reaching
out to touch
the small metal plates
identifying each bench by letter
A through Q
the back wall
bringing the alphabet to a sudden
end

the taped-over BB hole in the window
the constellation-like pattern of rug spots
the rusting fire extinguisher mount,
those are the landmarks
that kept me steady

in earlier years
we sat on P
until my brother and
i were respectively banished by my dad
to rows O and
Q
after a particularly noisy argument

and i stayed on Q
long after my brother fled
until the day my dad stopped pacing
could not be counted

and i left Q
moved up to D
because there was nowhere
further back
to go.

memorial board

rows of small rectangular
tarnished metal plaques
names and dates
clinging desperately to the peeling wall

there is no room here for flowers
amidst the blackened mini-bulbs
and empty sockets
tempting a child's finger
and a parent's scold

but the children and parents
caught on long ago
learned to avoid these places
where the books of memory
are heavy with scotch tape
blurring the hebrew letters
now indistinct as ghosts

still
on the board
the names are carved sharp
can be felt,
an errant edge can still cut

and so i pay my respects
searching out the extremes
the oldest and most recent
the longest and shortest lives
leaving my dad
for last

my gaze left
like the small stone

pinny bulman

laying silent, patient
on the distant judean hillside
that took him in.

before the eruv

there was a heaviness
to putting so much
down carrying nothing but
the key worn as tie
clip, belt tongue, the
bracelet she would pull when
i returned from shul her
tiny nose pressed against
the scratched up plastic door panes
straining to see beyond the building's
outer limits

started bringing her to shul
soon as she could walk the six blocks
most of our prayers focused
on somehow luring her
home without
a plaintive cry to be carried
insistent hands raised toward the distant
sky like a cranky prophet

in desperation we promised
unmissable adventures down each sidewalk
the building stoop where we pretended to be
statues unmoving until tickled
the storefront ramp she would fly down
to feel the wind in her hair
the cracks in the church steps teeming
with ants about whose lives
we would endlessly speculate

she squealed with delight the day i
showed her an ant crawling on my hand until
trying to help it back

pinny bulman

home i misjudged accidentally
crushed it,
we stared at the still twitching body
as her face fell with
the first realization that life ends
and some things once carried
can never be
put down.

corner church

the metal bars cemented into the top
of the high stone wall
needed to be gripped tightly
while peering through at the manicured lawn
bushes trimmed in the shape of a cross
that i'll always associate with a fear of falling

it became off-limits
when my dad started noticing broken bodies
that looked too familiar,
a dead boy drained of the libel blood
slowly lapping against the inside of the wall

but when i grew tall enough
all i saw were the cherry blossoms in spring
careless petals dotting a rustic wooden bench
as laughing children chased each other across the grass

and years later when my daughter
ran her fingers wonderingly against the rough surface
and then raised them toward the sky,
i picked her up and set her gently on the wall
where she turned her back
on my offered hand

easily balancing herself
she put her face against the bars
to see what was on
the other side.

pinny bulman

human shield

not so much a war
crime, more like two
grown kids playing street
tag except that one had a gun and
the other a look of
desperation as he crouched behind
my sister frozen
knuckles white on the handles of
the stroller where my niece
casually gnawed on a cookie from
the shul kiddush and eyed the man with
the gun, a smirk on her face that seemed to say
i dare you.

lights

columns of light switches
furrowed like aged foreheads
by decades of unwashed early morning fingers
thick with the bleary-eyed night spirits
who took refuge behind the panel
crossing the wires
until every flicked switch was an act
of uncertain faith

by the end
the only constant was the red glow
of the tiny bulb hanging precariously
from the cracked ceiling in front of the ark
the location of its switch lost
in the passing of the oral tradition to lesser generations
or some say purposefully hidden
at the time of exile
eternally stuck in the on position

years later
its glass prison long shattered
in the shul's fall
that escaped glow still catches me off-guard
stalking me like history

one night last winter
walking with my daughter
it was suddenly there
disguised as a deflated helium balloon caught
in a low tree branch
fleetingly illuminated by the taillight
of a passing car

i shivered with recognition and

started to point it out but
by the time she turned to look
there was already nothing left
to see.

sapling

i took the stairs slow
that last time
fingering the familiar nicks in the metal handrail
barely shadowed
by the sapling recently planted
in a final attempt at landscaping
putting down roots

i couldn't look it in the eye
glanced instead toward the demolition
notice scotchtaped to
the wall, one loose
corner shaking crazy in the wind
screaming *THE END IS
NEAR!* like some
untucked street preacher
as the branches continued
quietly swaying.

pinny bulman

reading cracks

hands reading cracks in the brick façade
following the undergraffiti palm lines where
a worn building's braille inverts into
an ancient stone hebrew of permanence crumbling
that once meant home

but my nomadic
hands can not
keep still,
feel themselves raw
rubbing against seasons that meant something once
about pilgrimage cycles
movement with
destination

until the past became a city overturned
and all of us
Lot's wife running from
that one final salty glance
back

so as the outer walls begin their slow silent fall
there is no encircling army
no trumpets blow,
it's just me and the cracks
translating ourselves into prayer notes
with no return address

just one last uneven fumbled caress
and then walk away
hands jammed into pockets where
little pieces of memory ball like lint and
fail to come out in the wash.

final sign on the door

there is nothing
worthwhile breaking
in here for. old
books, clothing and
garbage. the alarm
might still be on.
i hope you can
read this.

burn

no one knows how
the fire started
whether arson or
carelessly flicked cigarette

what is known
is that the burn of night
turned to ashy cloud
when the sun rose moody

and the stray cats yowled
keeping time with the car alarms
as the charred ruin
groaned its way down the street
and disappeared round the corner

a few years later
i walked by that garbage-strewn
lot overgrown with weeds
and watched two foxes
playing with a scrap of
singed tallis

until startled
by a rusty can blown
against the fence,
a sudden gust of wind
that carried a snatch of laughter
from the distance.

arrowhead

under the demolition rubble
an arrowhead
tip blunted
resting near
a fossilized piece of
churned up earth
mixed with bone

history whispering,
long ago
among the forest trees
near the riverbank
something big was
brought down
still kicking as it
fell.

pinny bulman

deconsecration

there is no
shofar blown
no candles lit
there are no
elaborate ceremonies of
holy objects shaken or paraded
no ancient prayers read backwards
in mournful melody

one day it just
ends

and the next time
i return
the star of david is semi-
obscured by a sign advertising a
sale on platanos
and the ghostly discoloration
of hebrew lettering removed
from above the
front entrance now
overlooks a gap-toothed
woman behind a stained card table
loudly selling
packs of men's underwear
for a peso.

jerusalem

the huge stones of these
ancient prayer spaces
press down heavily with
the weight of forgotten sacrifice,
worship measured in millennium
interrupted by
the occasional sabbatical centuries
the groaning relief of exile,
to these places
the dead shul across
the ocean barely existed
a hundred-year-old fruit fly

according to tradition
a newborn who dies
is like a stillbirth
the mourner's kaddish is not said,
but i will not be silenced
my prayer will echo
off these indifferent stones
if only for
a moment.

flood

there was no ark
when everything melted
rose deep into the clear sky

trapping an air bubble
in heavy silence
beneath the old barnacled shulwreck

someone's final sigh
a moment of letting go
submerged for waterlogged centuries

until the earth shrugged
and the freed breath
rose like a dove
to an unknown surface.

ear to the ground

the mystics agree about death
that it happens,
sometimes often

and the dead decompose
no matter
how tightly held or
which psalms uttered

except for a small
piece of backbone
that remains

a skeletal seed
lying in wait
to burst forth fully formed
at the end of days

and join the dazed naked
masses still reeling
from the awakening smack

lining up to board the old shuls
they too newly reborn
freshly dilapidated

waiting for a shift in the wind
to leap up
surprisingly nimble
and take flight
in migratory flocks
heading east with the storm clouds,

now i'm no mystic

pinny bulman

don't have the imagination
but sometimes when riding the subway
i feel a subtle tremor
rising up from beneath the tunnels,
something stirring below

so when spoken to
i may look like i'm listening
but i always try to keep one ear
close to the ground.

2: beyond the shul

rising

before the syringe dropbox was put up
as a mezuzah at the park's entrance
protecting the rusting car skeletons dotting the landscape
like picked-over carcasses,
this was a forest's edge

and in this spot
where you stubbornly refuse my help to stand
on legs still shaky
a bush once grew where a black bear
foraged for berries
as a doe and her two fawns weaved quietly
through the trees
on their way down to the river

yes, the same river that will one day cover all this
submerging our hubris in heavy silence
refracting our limits under a surface
masquerading as sky

but today the squirrels
are chasing each other among the wildflowers
when you put your tiny hand in mine
and lead me forward
step by shaky step

and as we quietly weave
our way down the slope,
you look up at me as if to say,
the river is rising
let us go to greet it.

fort tryon

i knew the hidden parts
the way the afternoon sun slid
gentle fingers through the crumbling arcade
stroking a charred length of curved pipe
leaning against the wall like a tired question mark

the road that once connected to the highway
now shed pavement on the downward slope,
came through here as it made
one last push past the rusting car frame
before petering out with a sigh
surrendering to the patchy grass, the empty bottles

a voice could echo in that high-ceilinged intimacy
where so much came to rest,
daylight's fade transforming the arcade
into a stone seashell
holding the slow rhythmic breathing of the drowsy highway
the occasional startle of a passing train's wail
the restless pacing of the insomniac river.

swallowed

i walk the winter park late
listening for the fleeting
moment the unmarked ground releases a cry,
my small rebellions
swallowed here long ago

but this night even time itself
has frozen to stillness
hanging off the tree branches
translucent and sharp

so i close my eyes
to hear a beating heart and
somewhere far above
snow settling on a still hungry surface.

sledding

the park stairs hibernated
their sharp uneven edges snow-sheathed
dreaming of shorts weather
bare knees

we perched at the top
packed tight in an old plastic washtub
my gloved finger absentmindedly mapping
a crack in the swollen side

for a moment it was all permanent, still

the black iron bars with silver handrail
standing defiant in the packed snow,
the looming bridge
frozen steel stark against the winter sky

my life a series of such moments
each ending with a sudden kick
to the back of the tub.

pinny bulman

stroller

that night, the stroller seat filled with snow
burying the neon orange salamander
the purple birds, their stitched wings half-open
always about to take flight
toward the bridge lights twinkling above
like distant stars

why do we make wishes
on something that may not exist
by the time it reaches us,
falling into itself
sucking everything into the dark

later the sky cleared and the moon
reached down to gently touch the sleeping stroller snow
before moving up to quietly stroke
an old rip in the fabric
that blinded the grinning sun's left eye years ago
the hanging cloth uncovering an emptiness
that contained everything.

arctic

extremities have always been the first to go
how many fingers martyred
to a dream of reaching that northernmost hydrant
and lifting a hind leg to yellow that once vast expanse
we still picture as immutable
ageless and white as some polar painted jesus
to whom we pray for resurrection
even as we drive in the nails

outside my window it's started to flurry
snow settling on a neighboring construction pit
cranes reaching their long slender necks toward the sky,
tomorrow the icicles will hang sharp from the fire escape
damocles swords over the street below
none of us looking up
until the first one falls.

melt

everything was steep there
even the river rising at an impossible angle
as we made our way to the tree clinging the edge
where the ground closed its eyes and
jumped

i was holding the two
candles we bought at the bodega, still blushing
from when the clerk winkingly misheard
handed me a condom twin-pack

they reminisced about a soviet childhood
roasting potatoes outside, buried in hot ash
but i was afraid of strange potatoes
foreign memories, borderless fires
the way they had of spreading

so we compromised
lit the candles and opened a bag of chips
whispered our stories so as not to disturb the ship lights
falling slowly toward the harbor

long ago when colossal glaciers slid through this place
gliding over its contours
that icy intimacy must have seemed it could last forever
but in the end when things melt
what we're left with are these carved out spaces
each with its own beauty of absence.

flagpole

the metal pole rattled
straining against its concrete base
as a nearby couple argued
one angrily gesturing while
the other leaned on the low wall overlooking the cloisters
her face hard and weathered as
the centuries-old monastery stones
restlessly skipped over an ocean's surface
to create an illusion of crushing permanence
where a unicorn trapped in tapestry will forever
desperately rear against hounds and spears
in a space heavy enough to contain our need
to kill even what we only imagine

a sudden loud clank from above
and we all looked up at the flag whipping against the sky
as though to say
i may be anchored here for now
but i will be seen,
i will be seen.

pinny bulman

gazebo

the word itself european aristocratic
planted on public television country estates in period dress,
this one the fallen american
out of wedlock scandal
gone to seed

we were warned not to play there
near the peek-a-boo pillars
that didn't hide quite enough

nearby a narrow dirt path led to a wilted fence
pretending to guard the rockface
that stumbled forward a few feet before
tripping into the underbrush

when the wind picked up
it fluttered the corner of a wrapper tucked into a crevasse
like a disposable prayer note, waving frantically
to the used condom stretched limp
unresponsive

the first drops fell silent
tentative
dotting the rock a darker grey

when i started back
the gazebo lifted its skirts
gave me a lewd laughing wink,
i hurried past
avoiding its sad gaze
in search of shelter before the skies opened.

underbridge

it wasn't so simple
to get down to that underbridge place
where the junkie tennis courts carpeted with used needles
lay cracked and dazed
near the river's edge

a small group from the nearby homeless shelter
passed around a tired volleyball
waved me over to a simple net strung between trees
this one fraying
like so many others

but holding on tightly enough
to catch us in the rhythmic back and
forth of ball hitting hand, head, air until pausing
to watch the sun fall
slowly toward the water

the river, it runs strong
said one of the men
like the river near my village in puerto rico where i
swam as a child
and he quietly began to remove his clothing as we warned
of toxic chemicals and swift currents

the game ending as he slipped into the river silencing
us as he swam way out past the shadows cast
by the steel towers of the indifferent gray bridge
shielding the traffic flowing rhythmically back and
forth, far above the little dead
lighthouse that stopped working long
ago when there was nothing left down there
that anyone still wanted to see.

to return

the metal sign wilts
tilts on its weary pole toward the river

                long since faceless

          struck
mute by the elements to which it now
slowly bows

        turning its back
to the rusty walkway over the tracks leading to
steps that crumble mid-
sky

     how does one descend
oneself when
devolution is not an option?

even the whales
          had to find a different way forward
to return.

nineveh

these shore rocks are still
slippery with life
discolored by clinging persistence, and i
run aground

the darkened lighthouse was once a tombstone
for this stretch of river
where you now work the edges
the warning in my mouth silenced
by a huge tail fin
alive and grey
momentarily breaking the water's surface

son, when you too are one day swallowed
do not allow yourself to be spit out
before asking
where is my nineveh?

beached

it was there when we exited the school bus
surrounded by police tape
laying on its side in a slowly expanding puddle of oil,
everyone evacuated except the pigeons
settling on the mammoth overturned tanker
like vultures on a metal carcass

temporarily homeless
we were each allowed to choose
a 25-cent bag of chips at the kosher bodega,
for years the most memorable aspect of that day

the smell of artificial barbeque spice on my fingers lingering
like the ghostly stain on an exit ramp
and the sound of a scraping match.

pliers

i wasn't taught how to make things
new, the toolbox itself with cracked
plastic hinge resting on the
slumped bookcase, a curbside rescue with exposed nails,
reading was never more dangerous

no, the tools i was given were
for living with brokenness

a hammer used to prop up the shade
with a few strategically placed toothpicks
in the rotting window frame,
and when we needed to change the tv channel
i ran to get the pliers.

pinny bulman

breakfast cereal, with roaches

1.
before taking the cereal box from the kitchen shelf
bang it twice with the back of your hand
then step back,
give the larger ones a chance to exit the box
and seek shelter

2.
choose a bright bowl with solid color
no patterned designs,
use hard plastic
or a startled jerk of disgust
may lead to shatter

3.
pour slowly and carefully in a brightly lit room,
always pour the cereal before
pouring the milk

4.
if you encounter one while eating
and your sibling gleefully repeats the joke
about protein being part of a balanced breakfast
say nothing,
use your spoon to silently catapult the roach
into their bowl

5.
even if your parents rarely allow sugary cereals
even if it is the only sugary cereal in the apartment
never ever choose the cocoa pebbles

6.
one day you will have a family of your own

live in a different neighborhood
you will forget that breakfast cereal once had roaches until
the morning the back of your hand accidentally
bangs the cereal box while reaching for the milk,
these memories will suddenly peek out over the top
skitter down the sides of the box
and while you sit frozen
quickly seek shelter back in the shadows.

pinny bulman

mime

neighbors drifted through
anonymous, noises bleeding
through the walls

few louder than
the mime in 1A beating
her daughter

we, tracing our invisible
limits, in the silence
that followed.

spices

the sages explain
that as the darkness churns
in shabbos's wake
the havdalah spices always carry
a consoling hint of fragrance
from the edenic garden,
even if the cloves were bought on sale
for $1.49 at the corner bodega
along with a quart of milk and the box of
off-brand trash bags that needed to be
returned because they didn't quite fit
the kitchen garbage

but even the most sacred spices
those burnt in the ancient temple
could not have masked
that saddest smell of transition
as our neighbor slowly decom-
posed in the apartment next door,
the lonely stench increasingly insistent
on announcing someone
no longer there.

pinny bulman

treasure

everything changed the day something caught
my brother's eye underneath
a car parked on our block
and kneeling down at the curb
he slid out an unmarked brown paper bag
filled with money

until that day, luck
meant not getting caught
stealing loose gum from the broken packages
at the bottom of the kosher bodega bin
but now i knew

those dusty maps with X-marked treasure
the winning scratch-off card
it was all true

and when my brother rolled
his new bike into the apartment
and parked it in our bedroom next to
the rusty dumpster dive we'd been sharing,
its red body was so indecently luscious
we crowded round
hungry to lick the smooth frame like a popsicle
and feel it paint our lips
coat our tongues.

knife

i never carried a knife
like the others,
didn't know how adolescence would end except
it wouldn't involve a sudden
display of combat skills

in a place where endings
were usually loud and flashy as
the bargain bins at Loco Loco
a knife could only whisper
a stain seeping into
sidewalk, i looked
away

and thought about the front pocket
of my cheap high school backpack,
how it already had a few holes,
pencils too sharp
for their own good.

near miss

a bottle shatters at 3am
same as it does any other time
if thrown from a passing car,
the rusting shopping cart doesn't startle
continues resting on its back
where sidewalk meets bridge

later the sun
will kiss each shard of glass
with bloody lips
but tonight all remains nameless,
a laugh fading with distance
my pounding heart
this bridge and the river rising below.

intersection

she danced slow
swaying mid-intersection eyes
closed to the blinkless cars slinking
through the sweaty hydrant underbrush
while high above my held
breath her arms stretched like night stirring
the long streamers of lotto tickets wrapping
the trees in a celebration of
misplaced dreams.

\

Bx9

ninety-two million miles later, the sunlight
slamming through the dirty bus window
projects urgent messages onto worn faces
become traveling destinations

an older woman humming softly
as she reads the gospel next
to a man with torn sneakers just conscious enough to
occasionally lift the spray bottle of dusting cleanser
to his nostril

all of us born in cosmic explosion, refugees
always speeding from our fiery origins,
stuck in traffic at unimaginable speeds

across from me a toddler slips a pacifier
over the bent neck
of a broken emergency handle,
one more child in this world deciding
to no longer be silenced.

kiko

you coming to the riots tonight?

it started with a smell in the air
when i left the subway
that mid-summer stink the neighborhood gave off
when it had one too many,
doused itself with gasoline
and began playing with a plastic lighter

or it started with two young men
one shot dead in a sweltering building lobby
the other holding a gun, speaking frantically
into a police radio

it started with the night lit up
by an overturned sedan burning
by the police helicopter searchlight
forced back to base by gunfire

it started with evacuating the preschoolers
from the day camp located a block from the precinct
under siege, as the only male counselor
they sent me to scope out the demonstrations, i stood
spanish-ignorant toward the back of the crowd
asked someone about the speakers, the chanting
he looked at me kindly, told me not to worry about details
just stand and listen

it started with a line of cops in riot gear
armored vehicles
scared shopowners with shotguns
the sound a body makes
falling off a rooftop

pinny bulman

it started with the shakedowns
the putdowns, the beatdowns
the crack-fueled community meltdowns
the burial mounds

it started with a question
called to me by a group of guys at the corner
on my way to rent a movie
for the campers still awaiting pickup

you coming to the riots tonight?

i stayed quiet and kept moving
as they realized their mistake, laughed
turned away

it started with a silence
with a question left unanswered

you coming to the riots tonight?

guilty

the side of an apartment building wasn't always long enough for the line of young men shoulder to shoulder told to go face it, put their hands on it, sometimes reminding me of a colonial barn raising except here it wasn't the wall in danger of falling. in our family stories from far-off countries, when a young jewish man was arrested it was usually for keeps. and if returned home alive, his little girl decades away from becoming my grandma, would not immediately recognize his broken body, hair turned suddenly white. but here the rules were different. pale as a ghost i floated past it all; the street life, the bodies, the line-ups, the cops. barely visible except for the occasional polite query. *excuse me, were you near the park when those shots were fired? see anything? alright then, stay safe.* until that one time walking home, noticing a car moving slowly, staying alongside me. two large men inside, eyeing me. that moment i realized the car was rolling backwards in the wrong direction down my one-way street. i was about to run when one of the men flashed a badge. *police! come here kid*, in a tone that had never before been directed at me. as i got closer i could see the undercover cops comparing me to a grainy picture of a suspect; skinny white kid, dark hair, glasses. the cop on the passenger side looked me hard in the eyes one last time before they drove away and i just stood there, heart pounding, knowing deep inside

i was guilty.

pinny bulman

street corner dominos

everything wobbled

the rough-edged square of thin plywood
                    set atop
the uneven stack of
                        empty milk crates

the pregnant paunches of the older men seated
            straining against
                    their yellowed sleeveless undershirts
with every laugh and
                    yelled profanity

the street itself through a liquor prism
                of glass bottles
        lifted to mouths by
                    shaky mottled hands

only the ebony dominos and their board
solid, absolute
carved from something once rooted deep
in a faraway place,
the sharp crack of each domino slapped down hard
echoing the sound of the first one to fall.

fire escape

when the city fell i
disguised my
self as a fire
escape clinging to brick, the siren
lights lashing red
on red on
red

windows nailed shut, too
fragile for passage or even reflection, i
held others trying to peer through
smearing the ash
when all that was really left
was the pounding, pounding,
pounding until there's nothing left to shatter.

pinny bulman

statue

the fire escapes here were all painted copper green
a reminder
that liberty's surface can change
corrode, like the old pennies
once thrown at me
in an insult i didn't
yet understand

but my grandparents knew
about always looking to find the nearest window to exit
about the way time could turn loss
into patina, a hardened shell
whose hollow interior i once climbed in grade school
to the crown where i stood looking east
from where we fled

on the ferry ride back i held tight
to my kippah shaking furiously
in the salty harbor wind.

smoke

so much of our memory in smoke
the ashtrays each a photo album,
we dip our hardboiled eggs
wondering at the faces hinted
in the patterns of grey on white,
ingesting a history
rising to air like morning mist
smearing the sun red across the sullen sky

no, don't feign surprise,
this was all known long ago,
the guard answering my grandmother
with a gesture toward smokestack
toward clouds growing pregnant
with all that's been lost,
and when they burst open...

shhhhh,
let's sit quietly on this cracked linoleum floor
and when you take your last drag
we will all watch the cigarette tip glow
like an autumn's final frantic flare
as i pass you back the ashtray

ashes to
ashes.

accordion

remember the night we sang
together on the bridge
rubbing our voices against each other
until i blushed and fell
silent?

silence too can be a gift but only
if chosen, with each fall
clutching its possibility of
rise

now i sit empty-
handed and through the screen i
watch your chest played by machine
like an accordion, roughly
squeezed again and
again as i cough up your name
and it quietly leaves the apartment unmasked
to wander the emptied city.

pretending

long ago we both pretended
to ignore the rats
running between our park bench
and the twilight harbor,
the smudged streetlamps
swept out by ocean current, i
tasted the salty end
heavy on my lips

let's pretend a fire escape on your window
a place to watch the hydrant mist
rise toward the muddy sky,
or let's pretend the window opens just a crack
no wider
a place to feel the locust
blowing east on a summer wind.

pinny bulman

thrashing

i can't seem to hold
my breath anymore,
hands busy feeling
the space of its absence,
attempting to communicate
through obscure dialects of pantomime,
shadow puppetry in the dark

i'm so tired
of languages
born of breathlessness,
i've become fluent in the last gasp
the fish on hook, thrashing

if we could just go back to catch
and release, our breath
rising into the sky like mist off the river,
all of us looking up with craned necks
quietly rocking back and forth
swaying in a prayer's breeze.

we used to buy umbrellas

we used to buy umbrellas
for two dollars at the bodega
their sharp metal spokes barely sheathed
in the cheap fabric
hungrily awaiting their chance to draw blood

that was before the rains
could peel off civilization like an old sticker,
roofs blown inside out
stuffed into all the corner trashcans

and the last umbrellas, twisted and broken,
have taken to the sky in flocks,
they perch on branches overlooking the bodies
no longer in need of shelter,
unable to see the rainbow slowly spreading
across the dark slick on the surface
of the rising water below.

pinny bulman

mars

even a planet can rust
if left out in the backyard
too long
vulnerable parts exposed

vast alien irrigation canals
coursing with water
reduced to optical illusion,
our anthropomorphic imagination dried and pressed
between the pages of old encyclopedias

and still we travel vast distances
to confront our old gods
in a near silence

searching for traces of
what might have been, while all that is
lies out back in the yard looking up at the night sky
wondering who will come searching
for traces of us.

copernicus

nothing remains still
as myths circle facts
like hunter and prey,
the center always
shifting, we stuck
in the first person
mostly singular
fingering the noose
we've slipped round our neck

after all if we can't be
the center of creation
there's always its opposite
looking beautiful from a distance
as most things do,
the sun itself a proof we now circle
that creation lies within destruction,
or is it the reverse?

pinny bulman

to that end

a friend recently told me
i use this expression often
a sly ironic shift away
from end to possibilities,
a series of personal deuteronomys,
whole scrolls filled with each word a sandbag
at the banks of the rivers styx
and jordan,
reminders that sometimes a promised land
is best viewed from the top of a far off mountain
because once seen up close
you can flee like trotsky to mexico
but ultimately you'll be feeding rabbits in the garden
just waiting for that pickaxe
to take you from behind
to that end.

hide and seek

long ago
the white tallis evolved
its black stripes
as a form of camouflage
allowing my ancestors
to hide within texts, the tradition
of techeiles intentionally misplaced
to avoid betrayal
by a flash of forgotten color

but history evolves too
playing its own versions of hide and seek
with colors that, once found,
bleed all over the sidewalk
and into the sky
where rainbows frown in a gesture
that once promised something

please, promise
something
before the evening wind
carries a final call of *olly olly oxen free*
each of us emerging from our fringes
our shrouds
holding a half coin
waiting to be counted.

come away

this summer night
the playground fences melt into the sidewalk
shrug off solidity
our liquefied longing greasing the swing chains
pooling in sweaty hands
the palm lines blurring
increasingly illegible

come away you whisper
let us cleanse ourselves in the hydrant spray
purifying this broken place,
listen to the lost harbor winds
playing the bridge suspension cables like a harp

i beg of you, do not awaken
the love until
it is desirous

we lean over the rusting railing
to watch ourselves ripple
in the river quietly cutting through the bedrock
itself vibrating
sending signals to something molten churning beneath,
why pretend that anything can be still
remain whole

come away you whisper
this water too can be split
and the wilderness pulled over our heads like a quilt
let us follow our pillar of fire
toward the distant spice mountains

come away.

Acknowledgments

The author expresses grateful acknowledgment to the publications in which the following poems have appeared or are forthcoming, some in alternate versions. When a poem has appeared in more than one publication, the first is starred.

The Americas Poetry Festival of New York 2022 Multilingual Anthology (artepoética press): "Bx9," "breakfast cereal, with roaches"

The Americas Poetry Festival of New York 2022 website: "Bx9*," "breakfast cereal, with roaches*," "come away"

Bridging the Waters III (Korean Expatriate Literature & Cross-Cultural Communications): "fort tryon," "pliers"

Culture & Identity, Vol. 2 (The Poet): "facing west," "jerusalem*," "swastika"

CUNY School of Labor and Urban Studies blog: "deconsecration," "shadows"

Escape Wheel (great weather for MEDIA): "mars*"

Family, Vol. 2 (The Poet): "havdalah"

The Forward: "hanging on," "leaking," "minyan," "pacing," "shadows*," "sign"

Jewish Currents: "blessing the moon," "ear to the ground"

The London Reader: "we used to buy umbrellas," "mars"

Mima'amakim: "minyan*," "startle"

Muddy River Poetry Review: "rising*," "swallowed"

NYC Poetry Magazine: "we used to buy umbrellas*"

The Poet Magazine (featured poem): "jerusalem," "mime"

Poetica Magazine and Award Collections 2013, 2016: "first love," "memorial board," "sukkah," "deconsecration*," "rock," "smelling salts"

Poetry Quarterly: "arrowhead"

the poet's billow: "to return"

Pressenza International: "impr0v1sati0n"

Red Paint Hill Poetry Journal: "trees"

San Pedro River Review: "pretending"

Songs of Eretz Poetry Review: "statue"

The Subterranean Quarterly: "burn"

Undeniable: Writers Respond to Climate Change (Alternating Current Press): "rising"

World to Come (Blue Thread Books and Music): "ear to the ground*"

About the Author

Pinny Bulman is a Bronx Council on the Arts BRIO award-winning poet. He has been winner of the Poets of NYC Contest, recipient of several ADR Poetry Awards, and a finalist for the Raynes Poetry Prize. His poems have been anthologized, including in the forthcoming *The Americas Poetry Festival of New York 2022 Multilingual Anthology* (artepoética press, 2022) and in Korean translation for *Bridging the Waters III* (Korean Expatriate Literature & Cross-Cultural Communications, 2020). Additional literary publications include *San Pedro River Review, great weather for MEDIA, The London Reader, Artemis, Muddy River Poetry Review, Red Paint Hill, Jewish Currents,* and *Poetry Quarterly,* among others.

Pinny was born and raised in Washington Heights, NYC, a neighborhood that continues to haunt his poetry. His "old shul" was the Washington Heights Congregation when it stood at 179th Street and Pinehurst Avenue, next to the entrance ramp of the George Washington Bridge. He currently lives in the Riverdale section of the Bronx with his wife and two children. When not writing poetry, Pinny works as a pediatric psychologist at a Montefiore integrated primary care clinic in the Bronx.

The Jewish Poetry Project

jpoetry.us

Ben Yehuda Press

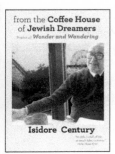

From the Coffee House of Jewish Dreamers: Poems of Wonder and Wandering and the Weekly Torah Portion by Isidore Century

"Isidore Century is a wonderful poet. His poems are funny, deeply observed, without pretension." – *The Jewish Week*

The House at the Center of the World: Poetic Midrash on Sacred Space by Abe Mezrich

"Direct and accessible, Mezrich's midrashic poems often tease profound meaning out of his chosen Torah texts. These poems remind us that our Creator is forgiving, that the spiritual and physical can inform one another, and that the supernatural can be carried into the everyday."
—Yehoshua November, author of *God's Optimism*

we who desire: Poems and Torah riffs by Sue Swartz

"Sue Swartz does magnificent acrobatics with the Torah. She takes the English that's become staid and boring, and adds something that's new and strange and exciting. These are poems that leave a taste in your mouth, and you walk away from them thinking, what did I just read? Oh, yeah. It's the Bible."
—Matthue Roth, author of *Yom Kippur A Go-Go*

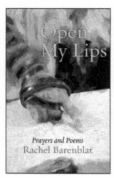

Open My Lips: Prayers and Poems
by Rachel Barenblat

"Barenblat's God is a personal God—one who lets her cry on His shoulder, and who rocks her like a colicky baby. These poems bridge the gap between the ineffable and the human. This collection will bring comfort to those with a religion of their own, as well as those seeking a relationship with some kind of higher power."
—Satya Robyn, author of *The Most Beautiful Thing*

Words for Blessing the World: Poems in Hebrew and English by Herbert J. Levine

"These writings express a profoundly earth-based theology in a language that is clear and comprehensible. These are works to study and learn from."
—Rodger Kamenetz, author of *The Jew in the Lotus*

Shiva Moon: Poems by Maxine Silverman

"The poems, deeply felt, are spare, spoken in a quiet but compelling voice, as if we were listening in to her inner life. This book is a precious record of the transformation saying Kaddish can bring."
—Howard Schwartz, author of *The Library of Dreams*

is: heretical Jewish blessings and poems by Yaakov Moshe (Jay Michaelson)

"Finally, Torah that speaks to and through the lives we are actually living: expanding the tent of holiness to embrace what has been cast out, elevating what has been kept down, advancing what has been held back, reveling in questions, revealing contradictions."
—Eden Pearlstein, aka eprhyme

Texts to the Holy: Poems
by Rachel Barenblat

"These poems are remarkable, radiating a love of God that is full bodied, innocent, raw, pulsating, hot, drunk. I can hardly fathom their faith but am grateful for the vistas they open. I will sit with them, and invite you to do the same."
—Merle Feld, author of *A Spiritual Life*

The Sabbath Bee: Love Songs to Shabbat
by Wilhelmina Gottschalk

"Torah, say our sages, has seventy faces. As these prose poems reveal, so too does Shabbat. Here we meet Shabbat as familiar housemate, as the child whose presence transforms a family, as a spreading tree, as an annoying friend who insists on being celebrated, as a woman, as a man, as a bee, as the ocean."
—Rachel Barenblat, author of *The Velveteen Rabbi's Haggadah*

All the Holes Line Up: Poems and Translations
by Zackary Sholem Berger

"Spare and precise, Berger's poems gaze unflinchingly at—but also celebrate—human imperfection in its many forms. And what a delight that Berger also includes in this collection a handful of his resonant translations of some of the great Yiddish poets." —Yehoshua November, author of *God's Optimism* and *Two World Exist*

How to Bless the New Moon:
Songs of the Sovereign and the Icon
by Rachel Kann

"Rachel Kann is a master wordsmith. Her poems are rich in content, packed with life's wisdom and imbued with soul. May this collection of her work enable more of the world to enjoy her offerings."
—Sarah Yehudit Schneider, author of *You Are What You Hate* and *Kabbalistic Writings on the Nature of Masculine and Feminine*

Into My Garden
by David Caplan

"The beauty of Caplan's book is that it is not polemical. It does not set out to win an argument or ask you whether you've put your tefillin on today. These gentle poems invite the reader into one person's profound, ambiguous religious experience."
— *The Jewish Review of Books*

Between the Mountain and the Land is the Lesson: Poetic Midrash on Sacred Community
by Abe Mezrich

"Abe Mezrich cuts straight back to the roots of the Midrashic tradition, sermonizing as a poet, rather than idealogue. Best of all, Abe knows how to ask questions and avoid the obvious answers."
—Jake Marmer, author of *Jazz Talmud*

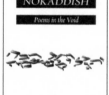

NOKADDISH: Poems in the Void
by Hanoch Guy Kaner

"A subversive, midrashic play with meanings–specifically Jewish meanings, and then the reversal and negation of these meanings."
—Robert G. Margolis

An Added Soul: Poems for a New Old Religion
by Herbert J. Levine

"These poems are remarkable, radiating a love of God that is full bodied, innocent, raw, pulsating, hot, drunk. I can hardly fathom their faith but am grateful for the vistas they open. I will sit with them, and invite you to do the same."
—Merle Feld, author of *A Spiritual Life*.

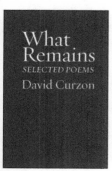

What Remains
by David Curzon

"Aphoristic, ekphrastic, and precise revelations animate WHAT REMAINS. In his stunning rewriting of Psalm 1 and other biblical passages, Curzon shows himself to be a fabricator, a collector, and an heir to the literature, arts, and wisdom traditions of the planet."
—Alicia Ostriker, author of *The Volcano and After*

The Shortest Skirt in Shul
by Sass Oron

"These poems exuberantly explore gender, Torah, the masks we wear, and the way our bodies (and the ways we wear them) at once threaten stable narratives, and offer the kind of liberation that saves our lives."
—Alicia Jo Rabins, author of *Divinity School*, composer of *Girls In Trouble*

Walking Triptychs
by Ilya Gutner

These are poems from when I walked about Shanghai and thought about the meaning of the Holocaust.

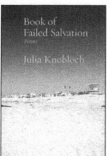

Book of Failed Salvation
by Julia Knobloch

"These beautiful poems express a tender longing for spiritual, physical, and emotional connection. They detail a life in movement—across distances, faith, love, and doubt."
—David Caplan, author of *Into My Garden*

Daily Blessings: Poems on Tractate Berakhot
by Hillel Broder

"Hillel Broder does not just write poetry about the Talmud; he also draws out the Talmud's poetry, finding lyricism amidst legality and re-setting the Talmud's rich images like precious gems in end-stopped lines of verse."
—Ilana Kurshan, author of *If All the Seas Were Ink*

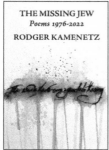

The Missing Jew: Poems 1976-2022
by Rodger Kamenetz

"How does Rodger Kamenetz manage to have so singular a voice and at the same time precisely encapsulate the world view of an entire generation (also mine) of text-hungry American Jews born in the middle of the twentieth century?"
—Jacqueline Osherow, author of *Ultimatum from Paradise* and *My Lookalike at the Krishna Temple: Poems*

The Red Door: A dark fairy tale told in poems
by Shawn C. Harris

"THE RED DOOR, like its poet author Shawn C. Harris, transcends genres and identities. It is an exploration in crossing worlds. It brings together poetry and story telling, imagery and life events, spirit and body, the real and the fantastic, Jewish past and Jewish present, to spin one tale."
—Einat Wilf, author of *The War of Return*

The Matter of Families
by Robert H. Deluty

"Robert Deluty's career-spanning collection of New and Selected poems captures the essence of his work: the power of love, joy, and connection, all tied together with the poet's glorious sense of humor. This book is Deluty's masterpiece."
—Richard M. Berlin, M.D., author of *Freud on My Couch*

The Five Books of Limericks
by Rhonda Rosenheck

"A biblical commentary that is truly unique. Each chapter of the Torah is distilled into its own limerick, leading the reader to reconsider the meaning of the original text, and opening avenues for interpretation that are both fun and insightful."
—Rabbi Hillel Norry

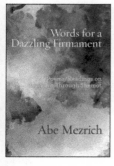

Bits and Pieces
by Edward Pomerantz

"A stunning tapestry of family life in the 40s and 50s. Like all great poetry, Pomerantz's work expands after reading. Each poem is exquisitely structured, often with a stunning ending, into a masterful whole."
—Alan Ziegler, editor of SHORT: An International Anthology

Words for a Dazzling Firmament: Poems/ Readings on Bereishit Through Shemot
by Abe Mezrich

"Mezrich is a cultivated craftsman— interpretively astute, sonically deliberate, and spiritually cunning."
—Zohar Atkins, author of Nineveh

Everything Thaws
by R. B. Lemberg

"Full of glacier-sharp truths, and moments revealed between words like bodies beneath melting permafrost. As it becomes increasingly plain how deeply our world is shaped by war and climate change and grief and anger, articulating that shape feels urgent and necessary and painful and healing."
—Ruthanna Emrys, author of A Half-Built Garden

Ode to the Dove
An illustrated, bilingual edition of
a Yiddish poem by Abraham Sutzkever
Zackary Sholem Berger, translator
Liora Ostroff, Illustrator

"An elegant volume for lovers of poetry."
—Justin Cammy, translator of *Sutzkever, From the Vilna Ghetto to Nuremberg: Memoir and Testimony*

Poems for a Cartoon Mouse
by Andrew Burt

"Andrew Burt's poetry magnifies the vanishingly small line between danger and safety. This collection asks whether order is an illusion that veils chaos, or vice-versa, juxtaposing images from the Bible with animated films."
—Ari Shapiro, host of NPR's *All Things Considered*

Old Shul
by Pinny Bulman

"Nostalgia gives way to a tender theology, a softly chuckling illumination from within the heart of/as a beautiful, broken sanctuary, somehow both gritty and fragile, grimy and iridescent – not unlike faith itself."
—Jake Marmer, author of *Cosmic Diaspora*

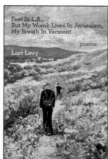

Feet In L.A., But My Womb Lives In Jerusalem, My Breath In Vermont
by Lori Levy

"Reading through Lori Levy's new book of poems takes my breath away. With no pretense whatsoever, they leap, alive, from the page until this reader felt as if she were living Levy's life. How does the author do it?"
—Mary Jo Balistreri, author of *Still*

Printed in the USA
CPSIA information can be obtained
at www.ICGtesting.com
JSHW081754101123
51574JS00003B/80